To Rosemary,

Best wishes!

Alan DeValerio

2023

A HISTORY OF ENTERTAINMENT IN THE

MODERN WHITE HOUSE

by

Former White House butler Alan DeValerio

THIS BOOK IS DEDICATED

TO THE MEMORY OF JOHN W. FICKLIN (1919-1984)

TABLE OF CONTENTS

INTRODUCTION

I was living in southern Florida in the late 1970s when I happened upon a book at the local library entitled **Upstairs at the White House**. It was written by J.B. West, who was the White House Chief Usher. All of the Executive Mansion's staff fall under the control of the Usher's Office. That includes butlers, maids, chefs, housemen, plumbers, electricians, gardeners, florists, etc. I read the book and found the account riveting. The White House staff caters to the whims of the First Families under which they serve on a daily basis. Sometimes a White House butler is the first– and last–person that the President or First Lady sees during the course of a day.

While I found West's book fascinating, I never dreamed at the time that I would someday be a small part of that legacy of service to the White House that was depicted in the book.

I came to Washington, DC in 1979 out of an interest in writing political humor. When I first arrived, I decided that I would need at least a part-time job immediately. During my college days, I had worked summers as a banquet waiter, so I applied for a part-time job with the Senate Restaurant on Capitol Hill. I would sometimes go by the White House to and from work, so, recalling how much I was interested in JB West's book, I decided to apply for a job there. With the aid of someone on my state senator's staff, I got the necessary governmental paperwork and filled out the forms. After being investigated by the FBI, I finally got the call from the Head Butler to work in December of 1980.

That was the beginning of my love affair with all things White House related. The White House is arguably the most famous address in the world. The White House is a superbly comfortable residence with 132 rooms, including bathrooms, archives and storerooms. There are three floors above ground level and a basement. The First Family's private quarters are on the second and third floors, where they sleep, eat their meals, and receive private guests and family members. Public occasions, ceremonies and banquets are held on the State Floors. The State Dining Room can accommodate seated dinners for 125 guests or standing receptions for up to 300 people. The Green Room, the Red Room, and the Blue Room can hold around 40 people comfortably. The main hall is used for receptions, and the entire floor can be used for events up to 1200 people. In summer, outdoor events can be attended by upwards of 3000 people. Everything that goes on at the White House is first class all the way! When the White House entertains, there is almost always a purpose to it, whether it is to curry favor with a particular group, reward donors, bring publicity to the President and his agenda or to showcase the Arts. An invitation to a Presidential function, regardless of one's political leanings, is highly coveted.

It is my hope that this book gives the reader a sense of how the Executive Mansion goes about the business of entertaining and how it has evolved over the years.

I: **STATE DINNERS**

Certainly the most elaborate, and the most costly, of all Presidential functions is the State dinner. It is a coordinated effort that involves everyone on the residence staff, from gardeners to maintenance men to florists to maids and butlers and kitchen staff. They require a tremendous amount of advanced planning and research. It is up to the protocol department to see to it that nothing is served that could generate the slightest of problems.

Visits from foreign dignitaries sometimes require months of advanced planning. No detail can be overlooked, from the need for interpreters, to various culinary and musical tastes. Even colors (particularly for flowers) are subject to advanced planning. In China, white is the color of mourning. In Japan and France, chrysanthemums are the traditional flowers of mourning. The consumption of alcohol is strictly prohibited by Muslim countries, but will it be awkward if it is served nonetheless?

State Dinners have evolved over the years, so what you might see at a State dinner today would in no way resemble what you would witness at a State dinner, say, during the Eisenhower administration. President Roosevelt did not host many State Dinners in the White House. He preferred to conduct Presidential functions at local hotels. The refurbishing of the White House during much of the Truman administration made White House entertaining impossible.

Democratic
Victory Dinner

March Fourth
1937

Mayflower Hotel
Washington, D.C.

Celebration

OF

THE PRESIDENT'S BIRTHDAY BALL

For the Prevention of Infantile Paralysis

Reception and Banquet

TO THE

VISITING STARS OF SCREEN, OPERA, STAGE AND RADIO

THE MAYFLOWER HOTEL

January 28, 1944

State dinner 1959

It wasn't until the Kennedy administration that the traditional round table that we see today came into use. The Kennedys also did away with the heavy, high-backed chairs and replaced them with smaller, lightweight gold-colored chairs that are still being used today (when the new chairs arrived at the White House, they were thoroughly inspected for flaws. However, the first time that they were used, there was a tack sticking up from the seat on one chair, and, as luck would have it, President Kennedy was the unfortunate person to sit on it!).

For me, the day of a State Dinner would start around 9 AM. First we would set up a tea service in the Blue Room. Following the welcome ceremony on the South Lawn, some of the guests would then come in for tea and pastries. Occasionally the First Lady would have a tea of her own in the Green Room. After tea service, we would begin setting up the tables in the State Dining Room. First, the housemen would roll in the round tables, then the maids would put the tablecloths on the tables and iron them. Then we would begin the set-up. The maitre d', Gene Allen, would bring up the large chest that contained the gold flatware. While he was doing that, we would go down to the basement storage and bring up dishes and glassware. The storage room was a treasure trove of White House china that White House memorabilia collectors would die to get into!

The table setting begins with what is called a base–or show–plate. (It has no function other than to hold the napkin and a menu card). When the first course is served, it is removed and replaced with the first course plate. After the base plate is put down (tables seat eight people), we would then place the goldware. Nearest to the base plate would be the third course utensils, which are the salad fork (on the left) and the salad knife (on the right). Then there would be the main course (usually meat) fork and knife and then the first course (usually fish) fork and knife. Then the glassware would be placed to the right of the utensils. Glassware consists of a water glass, a white wine glass, a red wine glass, and a champagne flute. The glasses that we used during the Reagan administration were initially purchased by the Kennedys. They are the only glasses that are replaceable.

Of course there were floral centerpieces and they were always exquisitely done. There would also be a small bowl with Godiva chocolates and another small bowl with mixed nuts. There would also be cigarettes on the table, although smoking was never permitted (cigarettes are no longer a part of the White House dinner settings). There were matchbooks on the table that said "President's House" on them. Along with the menu and program, they were a favorite souvenir of White House guests.

There were also side tables around the State Dining Room where dessert plates were set up. Each dessert plate had a cloth doily on it, and on top of that would be placed the finger bowl with water in it and a sprig of mint (grown on the roof of the White House). A dessert spoon and a dessert fork would be placed on the plate.

DINNER

Filet of Sole with Grapes
Fleurons

Suprême of Chicken in Tarragon
Wild Rice
Broccoli Flowers

Mixed Garden Salad
Reblochon Cheese

Watermelon filled with
Macédoine of Fresh Fruit
Biscuits sec

Johannisberg Riesling
Hagafen
1980 Kosher

Christian Brothers
Chardonnay
1978 Kosher

Schramsberg   THE WHITE HOUSE
Crémant Démi-sec   Wednesday, September 9, 1981
1979

The President

14

The author holding a Reagan China base plate

The President of the United States
and Mrs. Reagan
will greet
His Excellency
The President of the Islamic
Republic of Pakistan
and Begum Zia

10:00 a.m., Tuesday
December 7, 1982
at the White House

The President and First Lady greet the visiting head of state and spouse on the North Portico of the White House. After pictures are taken, they are then escorted upstairs to the family quarters where drinks and hors d'oeuvres are served. State dinner guests enter from the south end of the White House through the Diplomatic Reception Room and up the staircase that comes out into the front foyer. Drinks and hors d'oeuvres are served to the guests as they mingle throughout the State rooms. Then the President and First Lady and the visiting head of state and spouse are introduced as they descend the Grand Staircase to the sounds of "Hail To The Chief", and proceed into the East Room for the receiving line.

After guests go through the receiving line, they make their way down the hallway to the State Dining Room to be seated. There is a particular protocol involved with seating guests. Husbands and wives sit apart from each other to facilitate conversation (on only one occasion when I was working at the White House was this protocol not observed. The entertainment for that evening was blind pianist George Shearing. Because of his disability, he was allowed to sit with his wife in order for her to help him. A plate was made up beforehand for him, and when I served it to him, his wife, who was obviously impressed, said to him, "Oh, George, LOOK at that!")

All service done at that time was done in the style known as "butler service." A tray of food is presented to the guest, and it is up to the guest to then serve themselves with the serving utensils provided (This style of service has changed. Today all the food is pre-plated). Each table is assigned a host or hostess. Usually it is someone on the

President's staff or someone familiar with State Dinner protocol. Butlers were required to check their tables to determine who the host or hostess was, so that they knew with whom to begin service. Guests who were unfamiliar with what to do could just follow the lead of the host or hostess. Sometimes this could be somewhat awkward if the host was a man because many people have taken the mantra of "ladies first" too much to heart!

Dinners usually consisted of a fish course, followed by a main course (usually meat), followed by a salad course, then dessert. I was fortunate enough to work with pastry chef Roland Messnier. Roland was a genius at creating some of the most spectacular desserts imaginable!

The author with one of Roland Messnier's wonderful creations

Following the dinner, the President and the visiting head of state would give toasts. Then some of the members of the Marine Band would enter the State Dining Room and play a few tunes, or a singer would serenade the guests. The Marine Band has been attached to the White House since the time of Thomas Jefferson. Its no wonder that they are called "The President's Own." The band's uniform is red, with dark blue trousers with a red stripe down the outside leg, a white hat with a black band, a jacket closed with the brightly polished gilt buttons, and black braid for some and red for others.

Guests would then retreat to the State Rooms to be served coffee and liqueurs. They would then make their way into the East Room for the entertainment. After that, guests would again mingle in the State Rooms and be served champagne. The Marine Band would be playing in the foyer and there would be dancing. Once the President and First Lady retired, then the guests would be expected to leave. The Reagans did not stay up late and usually left the Sate Floor by 11:30PM (one of the full-time butlers told me that Lyndon Johnson was notorious for staying up late, sometimes to 2 or 2:30 in the morning. This was especially burdensome for this particular butler because he then had to be back around 7AM to serve the President his breakfast. On one of these late nights, he was so tired that he fell asleep at the wheel on his way home and drove off the road. Luckily he was not seriously injured, but he swore, at the point, that if Johnson was re-elected, he'd quit. Fortunately for him, Johnson chose not to run!)

Of all the State Dinners that I worked at, there are several that stand out in my mind. One night I had Frank Sinatra at my table and he was the host. Also at the same table was San Francisco 49ers quarterback Joe Montana. I could tell that Joe was a little nervous just by reading his body language, but he managed to persevere. Sinatra began regaling the women at the table with a story about how he once punched out a reporter and put him in the hospital. He then called the hospital to find out when the poor fellow was to be released. Not, mind you, out of sympathy. He wanted to punch him out again! The women seemed to gasp in what I could only hope was mock admiration. I thought the story was rather appalling, but I felt a little bit better about Ol' Blue Eyes a bit later when all the butlers were told that, if we finished our work in time, we were invited by Mr. Sinatra to come down to the East Room and listen to the entertainment. The entertainment that evening was Frank Sinatra and Perry Como!

On another occasion the host at my table was Itzhak Perlman, the famed violinist, who was also that night's entertainment. As I mentioned previously, both white wine and red wine was served at a State dinner, but for some reason we were serving two white wines that night. At one point during the dinner, Mr. Perlman asked me what the difference was between the two wines. While I must admit that I should have known, unfortunately I didn't. I couldn't fake it so I was honest. "I have no idea," I answered. Fortunately, Mr. Perlman just laughed. A short time later, while I happened to be standing near the table, one of the guests asked Mr. Perlman what he planned on playing that evening. He looked over at me and said, "Well, to paraphrase my friend here, I have no idea!" I could only smile in recognition.

Luncheon

Cold Chesapeake Crab Bisque
Cheese Twists

Escalopinis of Veal
in Marsala
Green Noodles
in Romano Cheese
Summer Vegetables

Raspberry Charlotte

Edna Valley
Pinot Noir
Vin Gris 1981

The White House
Wednesday, July 13, 1983

The 1983 Teachers of the Year

II: **RECEPTIONS AND LUNCHEONS**

Because the huge costs and preparations that go into a State Dinner make their numbers prohibitive, presidents sometimes have small working luncheons for various visiting heads of state instead. These are usually held in the State Dining Room or in the Blue Room on a long rectangular table that sits in the middle of the room.

The guests number around 15 to 20. For me these luncheons were a rare opportunity to listen in on policy talks. There are several of these working luncheons that President Reagan had that stand out in my mind. One time the president of Senegal visited. He stood around 7 feet tall and actually dwarfed the 6 foot 4 inch Reagan. On the other end of the spectrum, Israeli president Ytzhak Shamir was there one day, and he stood around 5 feet 4 inches tall. The two heads of state sit across from each other and there was usually a flower arrangement between them. In this case the arrangement was too high for Shamir to see over, so he attempted to move it. Unfortunately, he ended up knocking it over! Flower arrangement sizes shrunk considerably after that incident.

The most memorable working luncheon was when Andre Gromyko, the Russian ambassador to the United States, came to visit. It was the only time that Nancy Reagan came down to greet a head of state. The cold war was still being waged at that time, and she considered it imperative to make a point to Gromyko how important peace was between the two super powers.

The most ubiquitous of all presidential functions are White House receptions. You can expect, however, that no reception is ever held that doesn't have some underlying purpose. Oftentimes receptions are held for those who donate large sums of money to the presidential campaign. Fortunately taxpayers are not responsible for picking up the tab for these get-togethers, but the Executive Mansion makes for a nice venue when you are trying to woo potential donors! Receptions are held on the State floors (the East Room, the Blue Room, the Green Room, the Red Room, and the State Dining Room) and guests are allowed to mingle throughout. Sometimes hors d'oeuvres and drinks are passed and sometimes food tables and bars are set up for stationary service.

A butler carving a steamship round (1965)

Starting in 1978, the Kennedy Center has honored various performing artists each year, and, in accordance with those honors, the White House has hosted a reception prior to the Kennedy Center show. These events always proved to be great for celebrity watching as many movie, TV and stage personalities were on hand to enjoy the hospitality of the President and First Lady.

President and Mrs. Reagan with Hume Cronyn, Lucille Ball and Ray Charles

When President Reagan took office, his first official White House event was a reception for many of his Hollywood cronies. It was a star-studded event with a guest list that included just about anyone who was anyone in the world of show business: Jimmy Stewart, Charlton Heston, Bob Hope, Frank Sinatra, Ed McMahon, Johnny Carson, Ray Charles, Lew Rawls, Wayne Newton, Vin Scully and many others. When the President and Mrs. Reagan made their entrance and walked through the foyer to the East Room, the throng of celebrities followed. I was standing in the State Dining Room, which is at the opposite end from the East Room. I happened to notice that two of the guests, singer Tony Bennett and his wife, were lingering in front of the State Dining Room, waiting for the crowd to go into the East Room. They didn't realize that I was standing directly behind them. As they finally started to make their way towards the East Room, Mrs. Bennett reached around and playfully pinched her husband's bottom! What a great moment in White House entertainment history!

Another reception during the Reagan years that stands out in my mind centered on an exhibit at the Smithsonian called "Champions of American Sport." Many notable athletes were in town for the exhibit, so President Reagan hosted a reception for them at the White House. It was an amazing array of athletic greatness that gathered that day in the East Room. I remember seeing Muhammad Ali, Red

Auerbach, Yogi Berra, Bobby Orr, and Willie Mays, just to name a few. I was tending bar that afternoon and I quite suddenly found myself facing one of my all-time favorite athletes, Boston Celtics legend Bill Russell. He approached me to order a drink. Coincidentally, I had just finished reading his latest book entitled "Second Wind." Now I was very aware of the big man's reputation for being extremely aloof with the public. He never signs autographs. But because he had come to me and not the other way around, I figured I was in safe territory, so I said to him, "Mr. Russell, I just finished reading your book and I really enjoyed it." Russell just stared down at me and never moved a muscle. He took the drink from me, didn't bother to say thank you, and sauntered off into the crowd. I was very embarrassed until one of my co-workers made a comment. "That was pretty rude. You bought his book and put money in his pocket. You'd think he'd be a little more gracious." That made me feel a little bit better. Then I turned to my next customer. It was Oscar Robertson, perhaps one of the greatest all-around players in NBA history. He was very polite and well-mannered. It's interesting how people at the top can be so different.

There was another event at the White House that involved sports that I remember well. One year the National Hockey League was holding their all-star game in Washington, DC, so President Reagan hosted a luncheon to honor them. I'm not much of a hockey fan, but I was still somewhat disappointed when I found out that I wouldn't be assigned to that particular event. Instead I was to work a luncheon that Mabel "Muffy" Brandon, Nancy Reagan's social secretary, was hosting in the library for social secretaries from previous administrations. That event was running late and while we were waiting for Mrs. Brandon to show up, I had to go to the bathroom. I didn't want to travel the distance to the locker room, so I decided to use the guest bathroom just down the hall from the library. There was no one in there, fortunately, but just moments later after I had walked in, the door swung open who should walk in: none other than Bob Hope! I was so surprised that I became speechless! I may have managed a hello, I'm not sure. The irony of this story is that, when Mrs. Brandon finally appeared at the luncheon, she explained that she was late because of a greeting-line crasher: Bob Hope! Apparently he was in the line greeting guests when he wasn't supposed to be. What I found humorous was that all of the other social secretaries nodded their heads in acknowledgment. "That's typical," several of them said in unison!

III: <u>WHITE HOUSE BUTLERS</u>

Besides the kitchen staff, no other group of White House employees is more responsible for the success of a Presidential function than the butlers. From beginning to end, they are the face of White House entertaining. It was my great privilege to work with many full-time and contract butlers whose service went all the way back to the Roosevelt administration. Although they work behind the scenes, butlers are on a national and international stage as representatives of their country to other heads of state and foreign visitors. The best way that I can describe White House butlers is to say that they work with dignity and dedication. As former maitre d' Alonzo Fields once said, "I didn't feel like a servant to a man. I felt like I was a servant to my government, to my country."

White House butlers are a source of continuity as first families come and go over the decades. They are a valuable link between the past and the present. As John Johnson, a butler for over thirty years, says, "When a new administration comes in, they're just as in the dark as anybody else. They don't know what to do. So, as butlers, we have been there. We can kind of carry them along. We can help them along."

Far left: John Ficklin Second from left: Alonzo Fields (1947)

From left: John Ficklin, Eli Young, John Johnson, Gene Allen,
Wilson German (1971)

A group of butlers in the State Dining Room (1981)

The butler's pantry (1979)

When I first started working at the Executive Mansion, the Head Butler was a man by the name of Eugene Allen. Gene was one of the nicest people that I've ever known, and he is the subject of the hit movie "The Butler", starring Forrest Whitaker and Oprah Winfrey.

Gene Allen, the author and his son (1984)

Eugene Allen was born July 14, 1919, in Scottsville, Va. He worked as a waiter at the Homestead resort in Hot Springs, Va., and later at a country club in Washington. In 1952, he heard of a job opening at the White House and was hired as a "pantry man," washing dishes, stocking cabinets and shining silverware for $2,400 a year.

He became maitre d', the most prestigious position among White House butlers, under Ronald Reagan. During Mr. Allen's 34 years at the White House, some of the decisions that presidents made within earshot of him came to have a direct bearing on his life — and that of black America.

Gene Allen's predecessor was John Ficklin, who started working at the White House as a pantry boy in 1939. He was maitre d' when I began working at the Executive Mansion in 1980. By that time he was an iconic figure whose experiences were unparalleled. No book on the history of White House entertainment that covers administrations from Roosevelt to Reagan would be complete without a look back at the legacy of John Ficklin.

When Ficklin retired in 1983, I had the honor of interviewing him for a possible book on his extensive experiences. The project never got off the ground (Ficklin died of lung cancer a short time later), but it would be worthwhile to look back at some of the highlights of John Ficklin's career.

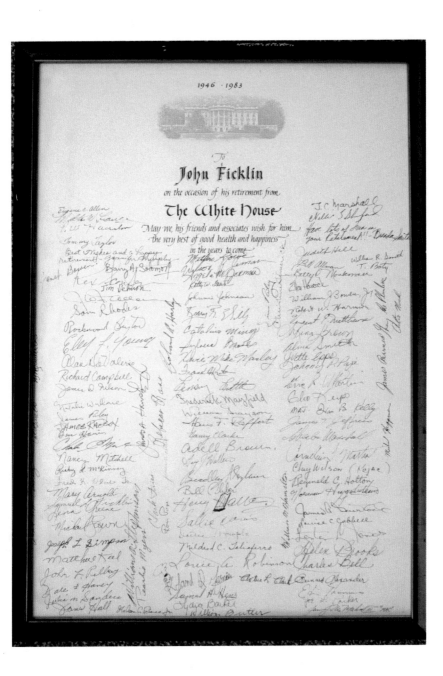

1946 · 1983

To
John Ficklin
on the occasion of his retirement from
The White House
May we, his friends and associates wish for him the very best of good health and happiness in the years to come

43

IV: <u>JOHN FICKLIN (1919-1984)</u>

He was one of ten children and he came to Washington, DC from Amissville, Va. at the age of 15 "to get out of the country." He went to work at a Silver Spring riding school and later as an office boy for a dentist. Though his brother Charles worked as a White House butler (and was John's predecessor as maitre d'), it never occurred to him that his own path would one day cross those of most of the major political figures of the mid-twentieth century.

He never kept a diary--"things I've read that some people have written, I don't know how they had time enough to hear and still be doing their jobs". But his memory was vivid and his recollections reveal that presidents and their families at home are pretty much like any other American families.

As the first person that they saw at breakfast and sometimes the last person they saw at night, Ficklin was given a view of real people and not just the polished image that the rest of the country was used to seeing.

For instance:

Harry and Bess Truman treated him like one of the family. Harry Truman knew everyone on the staff by their first names and took a personal interest in each one. Once

Bess Truman found out that John's brother Charles was ill so she had her own personal physician look at him. He had pneumonia and was subsequently rushed to the hospital where none other than Harry Truman himself went to visit him. He sat alone in the hospital room with Charles–no doctors, nurses or Secret Service agents.

President Eisenhower was the only president that Ficklin served who took an active interest in the menus. He enjoyed cooking (he would make soups in the third floor kitchen that Ficklin said were "pretty good") and barbequing (he had a grill on the roof of the White House). He made it easy for the butlers because he would set the daily menus himself, so there would be no conflict with a third party. He even made menu and wine decisions for State dinners.

Lyndon Johnson like to work late at night, but, when Lady Bird Johnson suggested to the Head Usher that food be left in the upstairs kitchen so that the butlers could leave at a decent time, they wouldn't hear of it. A late shift was added to accommodate the President.

When John Kennedy first came into office he made little attempt at learning the butler's names. Then one afternoon former President Eisenhower came to the White House to have lunch with Kennedy. Eisenhower knew everybody by their first names. Kennedy took note and soon after made an effort to learn their names himself.

Ficklin was at the White House when Mrs. Kennedy returned from Dallas. He remembers that she requested some hot tea and then she went upstairs to the family living quarters. She was still wearing the pink, blood-stained dress she wore to Dallas. She subsequently asked him to be an usher at the church (he was one of three ushers, the other two being Hugh Auchincloss and Washington Post editor Ben Bradlee), and asked that Charles accompany the family to the funeral. He remained at the White House for four straight days and only communicated with his family by telephone.

Ficklin knew two days before the world knew that President Nixon would be resigning. He was told to be ready to help start the packing.

Lyndon Johnson liked to drink scotch and soda, and each time he had a drink the bartender had to open a new bottle of soda–or else!

JFK, Jr. birthday party November 23, 1963

President, United States of America

Vice President, United States of America

Governor, State of Texas

TEXAS WELCOME DINNER

NOVEMBER 22, 1963, MUNICIPAL AUDITORIUM, AUSTIN, TEXAS

PROGRAM

Eugene M. Locke, Master of Ceremonies, Chairman, State Democratic Executive Committee

Music by Volunteers from The University of Texas Longhorn Band, Vincent R. DiNino, Director

Entrance of National and State Official Guests at Head Tables

Invocation by Dr. Robert Tate, Minister of the First Methodist Church of Austin

The National Anthem

Introduction of Members of the State Democratic Executive Committee by Eugene M. Locke

Introduction of Members of the Texas House of Representatives by Speaker Byron Tunnell

Introduction of Members of the Texas Senate by Lieutenant Governor Preston Smith

Introduction of Guests at Head Tables by Eugene M. Locke

Entrance of Governor and Mrs. John Connally

Entrance of Vice President and Mrs. Lyndon B. Johnson

Entrance of President and Mrs. John F. Kennedy

Welcome by Governor Connally

Remarks by Vice President Johnson

Address by President Kennedy

Benediction by the Very Reverend Edward C. Matocha, Chancellor of the Diocese of Texas

LYNDON B. JOHNSON

JOHN F. KENNEDY

JOHN CONNALLY

Courtesy of the John Ficklin memorabilia collection

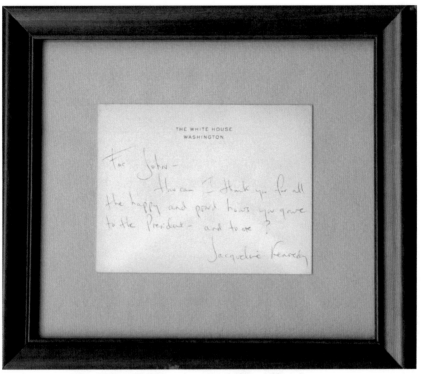

The John Ficklin memorabilia collection

There were throughout John Ficklin's career many, many events that took place on his watch, but a few do stand out above the rest. For instance, he presided over several weddings. One was Luci Johnson's marriage to Pat Nugent. Although Ficklin said that he got along all right with Lyndon Johnson, Johnson was a bit of a know-it-all who didn't like anyone telling him what to do. During the cake cutting ceremony, Johnson insisted on being right up there helping the bride and groom. It was impossible to attempt to tell the President that he was cutting the wrong layer. He was cutting into the cardboard part that the bakers used to support the multi-tierred cake. "I think Luci had to show him," said Ficklin.

To John Ficklin,

Many thanks to a real friend who really outdid himself at our wedding.

Chuck and Lynda Robb

51

Considering all of the events that Ficklin witnessed throughout his long career, there were relatively few mishaps that he can recall. One incident does stand out in his memory, however. Once a contract butler lit a fire in the State Dining Room without realizing that the fireplace was a non-working one. Smoke immediately began to pour out of the fireplace and permeate the dining room. Some guests began opening windows to air out the room. Ficklin recalls hearing Marjorie Merriweather Post shouting, " Oh, my God, the Lincoln portrait is ruined!" It wasn't, as it turned out, and someone was called in the next day to wipe off the smoke from the iconic portrait.

Because his career spanned such a long period of time, Ficklin saw not only many heads of state, but countless celebrities who came to visit the Executive Mansion. It was one of the perks of the job: getting to meet some of the famous from the arts, entertainment and sports worlds.

John Ficklin with Jack Dempsey (1966)

John Ficklin with Ella Fitzgerald (1981)

For John Ficklin – with thanks and good wishes – Julia Child

John Ficklin with Sugar Ray Leonard (1980)

John Ficklin escorts John Wayne and his wife to their table (1973)

As White House maitre d', Ficklin worked closely with both the President and First Lady in overseeing the myriad of events that took place from day to day, plus the everyday dining for the families who called the White House home. They each had their likes and dislikes and it was up to the butlers to cater to these whims (as it still is to this day).

The Carters eliminated the serving of alcohol from official White House functions, but they themselves enjoyed Rob Roys (scotch and sweet vermouth) on occasion. Eisenhower never served or ate anything other than American foods. He was the only president that Ficklin worked for who chose his own wines for state dinners.

President Reagan liked macaroni and cheese and occasionally would drink a vodka and orange juice. Mrs. Reagan kept a watchful eye on his dessert intake. Jackie Kennedy favored French cuisine. She didn't like a lot of decorations or garnishes on the plates. She thought that these items were only a way to mask bad food. Eisenhower, Ford and Carter would always eat in the family dining room on the second floor. Other presidents would sometimes eat on trays in their bedrooms. President Ford would usually eat alone and watch TV. Rosalynn Carter would sometimes join her husband for a meal and they would both read the newspaper.

If any problems occurred it was often the result of miss-communication between the First Family and the butler staff. Presidential aides were sometimes at fault for trying to read the President or First Lady's mind without consulting him or her. Carter aides ordered tons of champagne and wine for the inaugural parties, only to have it all sent back when the Carters made it clear that this was not what they wanted. The Fords weren't very demanding, according to Ficklin, and he appreciated the fact that Mrs. Ford would seek him out to tell him directly what she wanted. This eliminated any incorrect assumptions on anyone's part.

John Ficklin with Betty Ford

John Ficklin greets Richard Nixon at the White House (1981)

John Ficklin with Gerald Ford and Head Usher Rex Scouten

John Ficklin with Pat Nixon in the first floor Family Dining Room

John Ficklin with Pat Nixon in the second floor Family Dining Room

John Ficklin with Rosalynn Carter prior to a state dinner (1977)

For John Ficklin,
Best Wishes ———
Rosalynn Carter
Jimmy Carter

When the Richard Nixon came into office , the possibility of yet another White House wedding confronted the butler staff. White House weddings were a lot of work, Ficklin would admit, but they were fun too. Sure enough, Nixon's eldest daughter, Tricia, became engaged and married Edward Cox in 1971. Of course it was another grand affair for the Executive Mansion staff, but it certainly wasn't anything that they hadn't seen before. Richard Nixon was a bit more compliant as father of the bride than Lyndon Johnson had been!

Even though Tricia Nixon was somewhat of a private person, she chose the White House as her setting and invited around 400 guests. The ceremony took place on June 12, 1971 and was held in the Rose Garden.

While most White House functions, as I mentioned before, usually have a purpose to them, sometimes First Families just have something to celebrate. Birthdays come and go during the tenure of an administration. Sometimes they are small, private affairs and sometimes they are more elaborate. Such was the case in 1981 when Nancy Reagan had a bash to celebrate the President's birthday.

Throughout the years, John Ficklin garnered many accolades for his service to the White House, as the letter from President Nixon on John's 25th anniversary, and the letters from Lyndon Johnson and Jimmy Carter shown on the next few pages can attest. His dedication and service to the White House and all of the First Families was unparalleled.

February 10, 1971

Dear John:

Your twenty-fifth anniversary of service at the White House gives the Nixon family a perfect opportunity to express sentiments which we know are shared by all who have lived in this house for the last quarter-century.

The dedication you have poured into each day's duty and the sense of responsibility and good judgment you have always displayed have been as appreciated by those for whom you have worked as by their guests.

The knowledge that we can rely so completely on your abilities when it comes to extending our hospitality is a source of tremendous satisfaction for us.

We want you to know how much we rejoice in this milestone, and how much we hope that its observance will bring you as much pride as you have brought us.

Sincerely,

Richard Nixon

Mr. John Ficklin
Maitre d'Hotel
The White House

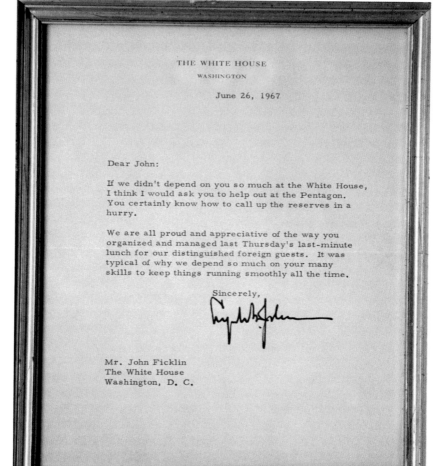

THE WHITE HOUSE

WASHINGTON

June 26, 1967

Dear John:

If we didn't depend on you so much at the White House,
I think I would ask you to help out at the Pentagon.
You certainly know how to call up the reserves in a
hurry.

We are all proud and appreciative of the way you
organized and managed last Thursday's last-minute
lunch for our distinguished foreign guests. It was
typical of why we depend so much on your many
skills to keep things running smoothly all the time.

Sincerely,

Lyndon B. Johnson

Mr. John Ficklin
The White House
Washington, D. C.

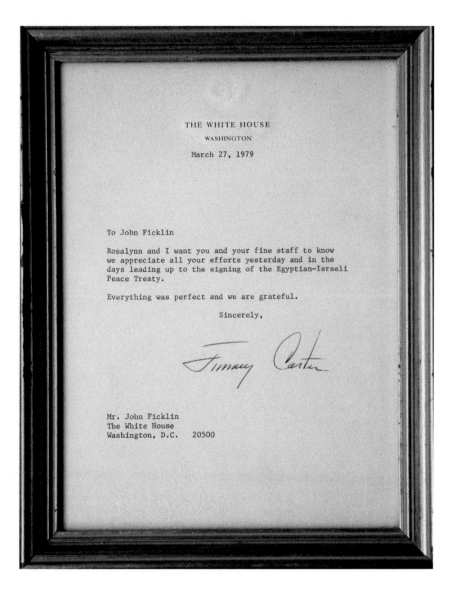

THE WHITE HOUSE
WASHINGTON

March 27, 1979

To John Ficklin

Rosalynn and I want you and your fine staff to know
we appreciate all your efforts yesterday and in the
days leading up to the signing of the Egyptian-Israeli
Peace Treaty.

Everything was perfect and we are grateful.

Sincerely,

Jimmy Carter

Mr. John Ficklin
The White House
Washington, D.C.   20500

71

No honor was greater, however, than the one that the President and Mrs. Reagan bestowed upon him just after he retired in 1982. On July 19, 1983, he and his wife Nancy were invited to be guests at a State dinner for the Amir of Bahrain. It marked the first time that a White House butler was afforded such an honor. It was so well deserved!

V: <u>HOLIDAYS</u>

From Easter to July 4th to Thanksgiving to Christmas, the White House has a long tradition of celebrating the various holidays throughout the calendar year. Some holidays come and go with little fanfare. Others are more intensely celebrated.

<u>EASTER EGG ROLL</u>

The original site of the Easter Monday Egg Roll was the grounds of the United States Capitol. By the mid 1870s, the egg rolling activities on the West Terraces had gained notoriety as the children turned the Capitol grounds into their Easter Monday playground. The first egg rolls, largely family affairs, seem to have been held during the administration of President Andrew Johnson. Youngsters of the President's family dyed eggs on Sunday for the Monday rolling, which the First Lady would watch from the South Portico. A family member has attested to hearing the stories of such activity from Andrew Johnson Patterson, the President's grandson, who lived at the White House while his mother served as White House hostess on behalf of her invalid mother, First Lady Eliza Johnson. Although small groups of egg rollers were reported on the White House grounds under the presidency of General Ulysses S. Grant, the majority of egg rolling activity and all day picnics took place at the Capitol. The workers and tourists watched in fascination as the children rolled both their hard boiled eggs and themselves down the lush green hills.

The egg roll activity of 1876 took its toll on the grounds, a fact that did not go unnoticed by members of Congress. With an already inadequate budget to complete the landscaping and maintenance of the grounds, Congress passed a law forbidding the Capitol grounds to be used as a children's playground. The law was to be enforced in 1877. But that Easter Monday rain poured down, canceling any outdoor activities sending the egg rollers indoors to play.

On Easter Saturday of 1878, a small announcement in the local press informed the egg rollers the new law would be enforced. President Rutherford B. Hayes, taking his daily walk, was approached by a number of young egg rollers who inquired about the possibilities of egg rolling on the South Lawn of the White House. Unfamiliar with the activity [his first Easter Monday as President had been rained out the proceeding year] President Hayes, upon his return to the White House, inquired amongst his staff who briefed the attentive Chief Executive. The smiling President issued an official order that should any children arrive to egg roll on Easter Monday, they were to be allowed to do so. That Monday, as children were being turned away from the Capitol grounds, word quickly spread to go to the White House!

President Hayes and his wife, Lucy, officially opened the White House grounds to the children of the area for egg rolling that Easter Monday. Successive Presidents continued the tradition, and the event has been held on the South Lawn ever since. The event has been canceled on occasion only because of poor weather conditions and during World War I and World War II. During the war years egg rollers were spotted on the grounds surrounding the Washington Monument, at the National Zoo, and even returning to the grounds surrounding the Capitol!

By the late 1800s such games as "Egg Picking," "Egg Ball," "Toss and Catch," and "Egg Croquet" were popular Easter Monday activities. The children attending the event take part in many newer activities, but rolling a hard-boiled egg across the lawn is still a highlight of the day. Presidents and First Ladies have personally greeted the egg rollers as have members of the Cabinet, athletes, musicians, celebrities from film, television, and theater and the official White House Easter Bunny. At the end of the day as egg rollers say goodbye, each receives a special presidential wooden egg complete with the signatures of the President and the First Lady and departs with fond memories of this happy tradition at the White House.

THE FOURTH OF JULY

July 4th doesn't have the same traditional significance as other holidays. Some presidents see fit to have a picnic on the South Lawn, as President Reagan did on several occasions when I worked there. Thomas Jefferson began the tradition of a public reception to celebrate the Fourth of July in 1801. The mansion was opened to all people. Tables pushed against the walls of the State Dining Room were filled with bowls of punch and plates of sweets. Presidents held these receptions until just after the Civil War. Ulysses S. Grant started a new trend for presidents in the late nineteenth century taking a summer vacation at the New Jersey seashore away from Washington's heat.

THANKSGIVING

Thanksgiving is another holiday that is not generally celebrated at the White House with any particular regularity. Its history dates back to the 1860s. New Hampshire author and editor Sara Josepha Hale, active in women's benevolent societies and well known as the socially influential editor of Godey's Lady's Book, petitioned Congress and five presidents to create a national holiday for Thanksgiving. Celebrating and giving thanks to the Creator for abundant autumn harvests was an established New England tradition by the mid-19th century. The governors of each state issued holiday proclamations that varied in date from state to state and from year to year. Mrs. Hale's long campaign to create a unified national Thanksgiving holiday met with success when President Abraham Lincoln recognized the symbolic wartime significance of the commemoration and signed a proclamation on October 3, 1863, establishing the last Thursday of November "as a day of Thanksgiving and Praise."

Today Americans continue to celebrate Thanksgiving on the Fourth Thursday of November each year and our presidents traditionally issue a formal proclamation of thanks. The tradition of "pardoning" White House turkeys has been traced to President Abraham Lincoln's clemency to a turkey recorded in an 1865 dispatch by White House reporter Noah Brooks who noted, "About a year before, a live turkey had been brought home for the Christmas dinner, but [Lincoln's son Tad] interceded in behalf of its life. . . . [Tad's] plea was admitted and the turkey's life spared."

CHRISTMAS

No other holiday is celebrated at the White House quite the way Christmas is celebrated. For me it was by far the busiest time of the year. There are seemingly endless rounds of parties at the Executive Mansion for everyone from Congress to journalists to military families to staff, etc. It was also a time for being able to enjoy the wonderful decorations apart from the usual long lines of tourists. One of several perks that we butlers enjoyed was being able to take as many pictures as we liked with our own cameras. Another perk was getting an official Christmas card every year. And it was also a time when we were able to pull some strings and invite family members to attend a Christmas party.

The author and his son 1984

The author's then-wife Vickie and Head Chef Henry Haller

Despite the fact that, during the twelve years that the Roosevelts occupied the White house, half were seasoned with war, Christmas was still a joyous and exciting time. Eleanor Roosevelt enjoyed gift giving so much that she even kept a diary, which she referred to as a Christmas Book, in which she recorded all the gifts that she had given over the years. It was kept right up until her death in 1962.

CHRISTMAS
1933

A MERRY CHRISTMAS
from
THE PRESIDENT
and MRS. ROOSEVELT

A MERRY CHRISTMAS
from
THE PRESIDENT AND MRS. ROOSEVELT

CHRISTMAS
1934

The first Christmas that the Trumans hosted as President and First Lady was the most memorable. It was 1945 and World War II had finally come to an end. It was indeed a festive occasion. For their first Christmas at the White House, the Trumans gave the staff a scroll of the V-E Day Proclamation with the new president's signature , and on December 22nd, President Truman sent Seasons Greetings to the thousands of members of the Armed Forces.

The White House was closed from November 1948 to

March of 1952 for renovations, so Christmas was celebrated at Blair House where the Trumans were living. For their Christmas gift to the staff in 1951, the President directed the Government Printing Office to produce 1000 copies of a photograph of Blair House taken by the Signal Corps. The gift was given to the staff by the President on December 22nd at his annual pre-Christmas reception.

Christmas Greetings from the President and Mrs. Truman

1951

White House – View from the East Garden

Christmas Greetings from
the President and Mrs. Truman, 1952

President Eisenhower took a personal interest in gifts and cards that were sent from the White House , perhaps more so than any other president. "Ike", despite having no formal training, was a very good artist. Six of his own creations were used as Christmas gifts to his staff during his administration.

During his first Christmas in the White House in 1953, Eisenhower referred to Hallmark President Joyce C. Hall for assistance with the first official White House Christmas card. An artist himself, Eisenhower painted a portrait of Abraham Lincoln while waiting for news on a Korean armistice. For inspiration, he used a photograph of Lincoln done by Alexander Gardner in 1863.

Eisenhower ordered 1,100 white keepsake folders from Hallmark, each containing a reproduction of his Lincoln painting. All of the folders were embossed with the official Presidential Seal. Over 500 of the reproductions were given to White House staff members at the annual Christmas party. Each folder was accompanied by a gift enclosure Christmas card imprinted with the words *"Season's Greetings"* in gold.

THE GREEN ROOM
THE WHITE HOUSE

When John Kennedy assumed office, First Lady Jacqueline Kennedy was amazed at the seeming lack of tradition and a sense of the history that had preceded them. She made it her mission to change that and make the Executive Mansion a "showcase of American art and history." Mrs. Kennedy certainly succeeded in her desire to call the nation's attention to the rich legacy of the White House.

Ever since that first official Christmas card in 1953, each administration has offered a Christmas card depicting many different scenes, usually White House related. The State Rooms were often the scene of choice from year to year. President Eisenhower was the only president to make prints of his own paintings for Christmas cards. Occasionally, photographs of the White House would be used, as in this Kennedy photo below taken by official Kennedy photographer Cecil Stoughton that was used in 1962.

With our appreciation and best wishes for a happy Christmas

John F. Kennedy Jacqueline Kennedy

The Kennedys first Christmas card (1961)

Possibly the rarest of all Christmas cards was one that was never sent. It was the 1963 card (see below). The President and First Lady signed less than 30 of them before departing for Dallas.

With best wishes
for a
Happy New Year

Crèche in East Room, The White House

Lyndon Johnson took office on November 22, 1963, following the tragic events in Dallas, Texas. It was just a month before Christmas. On December 23rd, the impetuous Johnson, understanding that life goes on despite the sadness the whole world felt at the time, decided at the last minute to invite members of Congress who still happened to be in town to a 5 o'clock reception at the White House. It seemed like an impossible task to the staff, but Johnson expected it to be done and it was.

As soon as the order came down, the kitchen staff jumped into action and began making finger sandwiches and arranging cookies and fruitcake on trays. The butlers began making tubs of punch and urns of coffee and calling in reinforcements. The White House state rooms were transformed as the black mourning crepe came down and was replaced by holly, wreaths and fresh flowers. A tree was placed in the Blue Room with a lighted nativity scene, and, with all the fireplaces lit, it created the perfect setting for the most impromptu Christmas party in White house history!

The Johnson's 1965 card

The Johnson's 1968 card

Today the White House is open to any and all tourists willing to brave the long lines and tour the state rooms with their myriad of decorations. This was a tradition that started with the Nixons. It was during the Nixon administration that the candlelight tours became open to the public. The exterior lighting of the White House was another tradition started by the Nixons. And the first ever gingerbread house dates back to that same period.

Gingerbread house 1983

Nixon Christmas card 1972

Just prior to Richard Nixon's resignation, Betty Ford was quoted in U.S. News and World Report as saying, "If I go there (White House), I'm going to make it fun. I couldn't stand to live there unless it were happy, free and open. Because we are that kind of people and we're not going to change." She lived up to her word! The atmosphere at the White House was simple and low key. Christmas during the Ford administration reflected that attitude of old fashioned folksiness.

NEW ENGLAND SNOW SCENE   GEORGE DURRIE (1820-1863)

Wishing you a Joyous Christmas and a Happy New Year
THE PRESIDENT AND MRS. FORD
1974

Like the Kennedys, President and Mrs. Carter were great American art aficionados. Jimmy Carter first became interested in art history as an education officer in the Navy. Once in the White House, the Carters realized that they had a wonderful opportunity to surround themselves with great works of art. Therefore, the Carters, to show their appreciation for being able to reside in the Executive Mansion, chose for their Christmas cards each year a painting of the President's House.

The President's House is a mid 19th century painting by an unknown artist which is part of the permanent collection of The White House and hangs in the Oval Office of the President.

The President's House

Jimmy Carter *Rosalynn Carter*

The four years that George and Barbara Bush (who met at a Christmas party in 1941) spent in the White House were marked by "firsts." They had the first holiday card done by a White House staff artist (director of graphics William Gemmell); the first card to showcase the Oval Office; the first card to reveal the family quarters at Christmas, and the first card depicting activities on the White House lawn during the lighting of the National Christmas Tree.

With best wishes for all the joy and peace of Christmas.

The President and Mrs. Bush
1989

With our warmest wishes for all the joys of Christmas
and peace in the new year.

The President and Mrs. Bush
1991

The Clintons, Bushes and Obamas have pretty much maintained the traditions of Christmas of their predecessors. They have chosen family photos for some years and depictions of various White House rooms and scenes for others.

THE WHITE HOUSE, THE RED ROOM, 1994

Our family wishes you and yours a joyful holiday season, and a new year blessed with health, happiness, and peace

Bill Clinton   Hillary Rodham Clinton

Bushes 2007 card

Happy Holidays

Wishing You and Your Family all the Joy of the Holiday Season
and the Hope that the New Year brings.

Barack, Michelle, Malia, and Sasha Obama

One of my favorite cards that I received during my time at the White House was one commissioned by President and Mrs. Reagan in 1981 and done by artist Jamie Wyeth, the grandson of N.C. Wyeth, who had provided the artwork for one of the Nixon's official Christmas cards. It is titled "Christmas Eve at the White House."

One of the thoughtful things that the President and Mrs. Reagan did during the many Christmas parties that were held every year was simply showing up to greet guests and sometimes sign autographs. Many thousands of people attend official White House Christmas functions and the President and his wife never failed to disappoint the throngs.

The President and Mrs. Reagan with the staff after last party of 1983

VI: <u>MEMORABLE EVENTS</u>

During the course of an administration, many events are held each year. Every administration hosts countless receptions, luncheons, private gatherings, performances and the like. However, there are some events that stand out above the others. When I first started to work at the White House, I liked to query the butlers who had been around for a long time on their memories. One event that kept coming up time and again was, ironically, an event that took place outside of the White House!

On July 11, 1961, the Kennedys held an elaborate State dinner (fancy even for State dinner standards) on Mount Vernon's East Lawn in honor of General Muhammad Ayub Khan, the president of Pakistan, a country that was an important ally to the United States during the Cold War era.

A thirty-by-fifty-foot tent that was blue on top and buttercup yellow on the underside went up on the East Lawn. Centerpieces of asters, baby's breath, blue delphiniums, yellow carnations, lemon lilies and blue bachelor's buttons were placed on the tables underneath. A bandstand for a post-dinner concert by the National Symphony Orchestra was set up across the lawn.

Guests arrived via boat at the Mount Vernon wharf, then toured Washington's home before sipping on bourbon mint juleps or frosted orange drinks (for the nondrinkers) on Washington's Piazza. Afterward the president and first lady escorted Ayub and his daughter, the Begum Nasir Aurangzeb, to the other side of the Mansion where fifty-four marines carrying state flags lined the roundabout. The Army's Colonial Color Guard and Fife and Drum Corps performed a reenactment of a Revolutionary War-era military drill.

The evening's meal consisted of French cuisine, which had to be transported from the White House. In 1961 there was no kitchen available for such a culinary feat at Mount Vernon, except perhaps Washington's original, no longer in commission even for the likes of Kennedy.

First Lady Jackie Kennedy wore a sleeveless white organza and lace evening gown, with a chartreuse silk sash. Ayub's daughter wore a white silk sari. It was truly a night worthy of the Washingtons.

There was another memorable event that stood out during the Kennedy administration. It was an official dinner that took place on November 13, 1961, in honor of Governor Luis Munoz Marin of Puerto Rico. In this case, it wasn't the person being honored that made it special. It was the evening's entertainment that came to typify the blend of social occasion and high art of the Kennedy administration. The after dinner entertainment was cellist Pablo Casals, who was playing at the White House for the first time since his 1904 performance for Theodore Roosevelt. The program was devoted entirely to serious chamber music, and the audience included virtually every well-known American composer, from Leonard Bernstein to Samuel Barber.

Another memorable event was the black tie dinner Richard Nixon gave 600 newly freed prisoners of North Vietnam on May 24, 1971. It was one of the biggest ever held in White House history. Technically, it was outside the White House on the South Lawn. The White House had to borrow two refrigerator vans from the army to keep the first course (Supreme of Seafood Neptune) and dessert (strawberry mousse) at precisely 36 degrees. Nixon also served the POWs the biggest names in entertainment: Jimmy Stewart, Bob Hope and John Wayne.

There are a couple of events that stand out in my mind that took place during my tenure. One was an event that President and Mrs. Carter hosted on December 22, 1980. A skating rink was erected on the South Lawn and Olympic gold medalist Peggy Fleming was brought in to perform. There was one performance in the afternoon and one in the evening. Food and drinks were served. Fortunately it wasn't a particularly cold day. All the butlers were issued heavy Army type pea coat jackets and gloves to wear with our tuxedo pants!

Fortunately it was a nice, bright sunny day and not too cold in the afternoon. I was working the food grill, so I had no problems keeping warm. At night, however, it was a different story. As the sun descended, so did the temperature. It was so cold that I saw a congressman with his hands in his own pockets!

Another problem for me was that I was no longer on the grill. Now I was serving hot chocolate. I couldn't wear the gloves that we had been provided because they were too bulky. My hands were so cold that I started pouring the hot chocolate on them to keep them warm. Well, as luck would have it, after the performance, President and Mrs. Carter came to my station for hot chocolate. And I had run out! So I had my big chance to serve the President and First Lady, and I blew it!

THE PRESIDENT AND MRS. CARTER

welcome you to

An Old Fashioned Christmas

THE WHITE HOUSE

Monday, December 22, 1980

Jimmy Carter

My signed program from that night

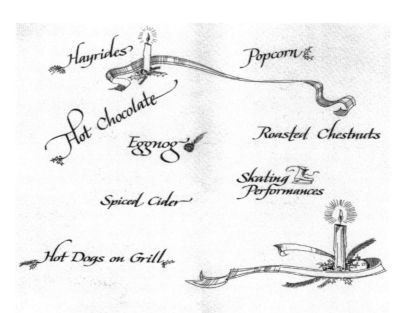

Hayrides

Popcorn

Hot chocolate

Eggnog

Roasted Chestnuts

Skating Performances

Spiced Cider

Hot Dogs on Grill

Program

Toy Soldiers on Parade
Barbara Russell   Amy Willard
Daryl Clougher   Lois Heath
Robert Strong

Partridge in a Pear Tree
Ron Urban

PEGGY FLEMING

Changing of the Guard
Jock and Margaret McConnell

A Lover's Fantasy
Charles and Dolores Younker

PEGGY FLEMING

Christmas Bird
Amy Willard

Space Cadet
Robert Strong

PEGGY FLEMING

Colonial Ball
Barbara Russell   Amy Willard
Daryl Clougher   Lois Heath
Robert Strong

Christmas with Santa
Barbara Russell   Amy Willard
Daryl Clougher   Lois Heath
Santa Claus

Finale
Ice Ensemble

Every year the White House hosts the nation's governors with a big dinner in January in conjunction with the Governor's Association meeting in Washington, DC. One year I was able to strike up a conversation with the governor of my home state of Rhode Island, J. Joseph Garrahy. Governor Garrahy was excited when I told him I was a native Rhode Islander, and I greatly enjoyed meeting him and his lovely wife Margherite. It was only afterwards that the thought occurred to me that I should have gotten the both of them to sign a menu for me. The next best thing to do would be to send them a menu in the mail and hope that they would sign and return it. I did just that and they were gracious enough to sign it for me.

As you can see from the letter that accompanied the menu, the Governor asked me to supply him with a copy of the menu. I guess they both forgot to take their menus with them. Fortunately, I was able to come up with one and gladly sent it to them. That was a special night for me and one that I always remember with fondness.

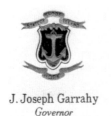

January 21, 1981

Mr. Alan DeValerio
3315 Wisconsin Avenue, N.W.
Apartment 607
Washington, DC 20016

Dear Alan:

It was so nice meeting you at the White House on
January 7 and it is with great pleasure that I am
returning the menu from that evening that Mrs.
Garrahy and I have signed.

I also like to keep mementos of important occasions,
and I was wondering if you would be able to obtain
a copy of the menu for me. If so, Mrs. Garrahy and
I will be very grateful.

Sincerely,

J. Joseph Garrahy
G O V E R N O R

Enclosure

114

DINNER

Striped Bass in Oyster Sauce
Fleurons

Roast Pheasant Smitane
Wild Rice
Broccoli Spears

Romaine Lettuce and Grapefruit Salad
Trappist Cheese

Orange Cake en Surprise
Sauce Grand Marnier

Ste. Michelle
Johannisberg Riesling

Simi Cabernet Sauvignon

Great Western
Natural Champagne

Margherita Lansky
Gov. J. Joseph Sarah, R.I.

One of the rewards for working at the White House as a butler was getting the opportunity to work in the family quarters on the second floor. I wish that, when people take the White House tours that are open to the public, they could see the upstairs. Living on the second floor would be tantamount to living in a museum. It is quite spectacular, not to mention incredibly historic. What a thrill it was for me to get to see the Queen's Room, the Lincoln Room, the President's bedroom, the Yellow Oval Room (the quintessential reception area overlooking the Truman Balcony) and my favorite, the Solarium (a very brightly decorated room that lives up to it's name as it is filled with sunshine most of the day).

Dinners upstairs were much different than downstairs dinners. The Family Dining Room is small (at least in comparison to the State rooms). Usually there would be four round tables with eight guests at each table. There is a kitchen off of the dining room. It looks like any kitchen that you would see in someone's home (the space was converted into a kitchen by Jackie Kennedy).

One occasion when we were working upstairs really stands out in my memory. It was a dinner for German Chancellor Helmut Kohl and his wife. We were setting up in the dining room around 4:30 or so when suddenly President Reagan and Mrs. Reagan walked in. I happened to be standing by the President's table as he sauntered over to see what guests were to be seated at his table. Just a few days prior the President and First Lady had signed a photo of me serving them at an outdoor event, so I thanked the President for doing that (I'm sure he had no idea what I was talking about!). He graciously said that he was glad to do it anytime. So there I was, chit chatting with the President of the United States in the family quarters—and getting paid to do it!

As it turned out, I was assigned to the President's table that night. There is a bit of prestige amongst the butlers that goes along with being assigned to serve the President (the butler on the President's table takes his cue from the maitre d' and then the other butlers take their cue from whoever is serving the President).

After dinner there is entertainment. This night it happened to be the wonderful Marvin Hamlisch. Try to imagine listening to Marvin Hamlisch playing "The Way We Were" on the piano in the Yellow Oval Room of the White House (and, once again, getting paid for it!) Priceless!

After the entertainment, we were to serve champagne to the guests. This is where the night almost ended in disaster. I was the first butler to come into the room with four champagne glasses (not flutes but the fruit cup type glasses) on a tray. Of course, the first people I was to serve would be the two heads of state and their wives. Most service of this type is done while guests are standing, but in this case they were sitting on one of the sofas. I now had to bend down to serve them, and I wasn't used to doing that.

As I bent down, the glasses suddenly started to slide off the tray! Fortunately, I didn't panic. I was able to upright the tray before the glasses slid off and landed in the laps of the two presidents and/or their spouses. I think I lost about five years off my life in that moment! To this day, anytime I see those fruit cup glasses, I break out in a cold sweat!

The Yellow Oval Room. The author is on the right

VII: SOCIAL SECRETARIES AND USHERS

The position of White House social secretary traces its origins to the employment of Isabella Hagner as a salaried executive clerk assigned to First Lady Edith Roosevelt in 1901. Before that time male clerks in the president's office assumed the duties of correspondence, invitation lists, seating charts, floral decorations, and menus usually under the direction of a presidential aide.

The newspapers in the early twentieth century often portrayed Belle Hagner as "arbiter of White House social affairs" or the "real social ruler at the White House." In reality, the changes to the social functions at the White House were a part of a larger reorganization of the house. President Theodore Roosevelt established the position of chief usher, an organizational chart for the 57 people working in and around the White House, and assigned a military aide to assist the president and first lady for more complex tasks. Roosevelt also brought military aides to the White House and at social events had the young military officers bedecked in dress uniforms to provide flair to any social occasion.

For more than one hundred years, White House Social Secretaries have been individuals with a tenacity of purpose, loyal to the president and first lady, and a profound knowledge of protocol and society in Washington, D.C. As time passed first ladies naturally expanded the number of staff working on social events. First Lady Grace Coolidge retained Laura Harlan, social secretary in the Harding administration, and added Mary

Randolph to her staff to work on social events. First Lady Eleanor Roosevelt handled the vast social side of the Roosevelt White House with the assistance of her personal secretary, Malvina "Tommy" Thompson and Edith Benham Helm.

First ladies have had a social secretary and clerks on the government payroll, but the positions were not recognized as part of the institutionalized presidency until the Eisenhower administration. Social Secretary Mary Jane McCaffree was listed in the Congressional Directory's top White House personnel as "Acting Secretary to the President's Wife." Today the social secretary also holds a position as a special assistant to the president.

Belle Hagner and stepson Alec

The social secretary works with the First Lady in the overall planning, arrangement, coordination and direction of all personal social events given by the president and his family. This includes the forming and wording of invitations, the compiling of guest lists, the setting of menus, the seating, the choice of decorations and the selection of entertainment.

There is no guidebook for social secretaries to follow. It is tradition for the current social secretary to host a luncheon for past social secretaries to get ideas and advice.

The social secretaries office is in charge of official guest lists for State dinners. After being notified of a dinner, the social secretary requests input from senior staff members to provide a list from their areas of expertise. There is an official party list from the State Department, and these lists are combined. The President and First Lady are consulted also, and another list of celebrities, cultural and academic figures, athletes and other persons of interest is added.

Changes in technology over the past century have greatly impacted the responsibilities of the social secretary. In the early twentieth century, the social secretary was responsible for answering hand-written correspondence and telephone calls. Since the advent of the internet, cell phones, and digital communication, the social secretary's job has become less encumbered with details and tied to the 24/7 news cycle and the increased prominence and scrutiny of the White House and the first family.

*Mabel "Muffy"Brandon, social
secretary to Nancy Reagan*

The White House Ushers Office is one of the most unique
working places in the world. Located adjacent to the
Entrance Hall, it has become a platform for witnessing
history. The main function of the office is to oversee the
official and domestic life of the First Families. The Head
Usher is a sort of general manager of the Executive
Mansion. The current Ushers Office runs a staff of seven,
which includes a chief usher, deputy chief usher, four

assistant ushers, and one executive assistant. The ushers work in shifts and manage official and ceremonial events ranging from formal State dinners to holiday receptions, and oversee a vast collection of fine and decorative arts. Basically, the White House is three buildings in one—a private home, a venue for events and a historic museum. The job title of Chief Usher was changed in 2007 to "director of the Executive Residence and Chief Usher."

John Ficklin (R) with Chief Usher Rex Scouten (1970)

FINAL THOUGHTS

The White House, over the years, has hosted many, many presidential functions. Although it is primarily the home of the First Family, the Executive Mansion plays an important role in the life of each and every administration. Successful State dinners, working luncheons and receptions can go a long way in establishing solid relationships for any president with his contemporaries, be they foreign or domestic. The importance of having a good staff, whether it's butlers, chefs or doormen, that can handle any contingency, cannot be stressed enough.

It is difficult to put into words what it was like working at the White House. The atmosphere is like no other anywhere. Imagine going to work every day with the knowledge that anyone in the world might be a visiting guest. I had a chance to talk about comedy writing with Carl Reiner. I talked about the Yankees with Yogi Berra. I chatted about one of my all-time favorite sit-coms, "All in the Family", with one of its stars, Sally Struthers (the nicest celebrity that I ever met at the White House). I got to hear Eubie Blake play the piano in the East Room, and I was at the White House in 1981 when three former presidents (Nixon, Ford and Carter), one current president (Reagan), and one future president (George H.W. Bush) were all in the same room.

It was also a great honor for me to be associated with all of the wonderful people that I was so fortunate to work with.

I can only hope that you have gotten from this book some small sense of what an overwhelming experience it truly was!

THE PRESIDENT AND MRS. CARTER
welcome you to
THE WHITE HOUSE
Monday, January 5, 1981

DINNER HONORING
Her Royal Highness The Princess Margaret
Countess of Snowdon

Maine Lobster en Gelée
Fines Herbes Sauce
Melba Toast Parmesan

Suprême of Chicken à l'Orange
Wild Rice with Almonds & Raisins
Artichoke Hearts St. Germain

Belgian Endive & Watercress Salad
with Goat Cheese

Sorbet en Surprise
Petits Fours

Hanzell Vineyards Chardonnay 1978
Schramsberg Crémant Demi-Sec 1979

THE WHITE HOUSE
Saturday, October 1, 1983

LUNCHEON

In celebration of the
Harry S. Truman Centennial

Minted Cantaloupe & Honeydew

Tenderloin of Veal
in Red Pepper
Spaetzle Noodles
Broccoli in Parmesan

Oranges Glacée Grand Marnier
Petits Fours

Sanford Pinot Noir-Vin Gris 1983

THE WHITE HOUSE
Tuesday, May 8, 1984

The Presidential Inaugural Committee
requests the honor of your presence
to attend and participate in the Inauguration of

Ronald Wilson Reagan

as President of the United States of America
and

George Herbert Walker Bush

as Vice President of the United States of America
on Tuesday the twentieth of January
one thousand nine hundred and eighty one
in the City of Washington

CONGRESSIONAL BARBECUE
THE WHITE HOUSE
September 30, 1982

ABOUT THE AUTHOR

Alan DeValerio is a native Rhode Islander but Maryland has been home for over 30 years. He began working at the White House in 1980 as a contract butler and worked there until the beginning of the first Bush administration. He is currently writing an article about the White House for Washingtonian magazine and in the spring of 2015 he will be writing another for the White House Historical Association. He does a presentation on his experiences called "At Your Service, Mr. President."

For more information visit:
www.whitehousememories.com

Made in the USA
Middletown, DE
01 April 2023

27846274R00075